Cyber Security Advanced

About

With a distinguished background as a veteran of the UK Armed Forces, this author brings over 23 years of expertise in the field of cyber security. Having served both independently and within prominent organizations, they have dedicated their career to providing top-notch cyber security services to local and central government departments. Their unique blend of military discipline and deep industry knowledge positions them as a formidable authority on safeguarding digital landscapes, making complex concepts accessible and engaging for a wide audience.

Table of Contents

1. Introduction to Cyber Security

(1) - 1.1 The Importance of Cyber Security in 2025

(2) - 1.2 Overview of Cyber Threats

(3) - 1.3 Cyber Security Frameworks and Standards

2. Understanding Threat Landscapes

(1) - 2.1 Types of Cyber Threats and Vulnerabilities

(2) - 2.2 Emerging Threat Trends

(3) - 2.3 Real-World Case Studies of Cyber Attacks

3. Network Security Fundamentals

(1) - 3.1 Essential Network Security Concepts

(2) - 3.2 Firewalls, IDS/IPS, and Their Roles

(3) - 3.3 Securing Network Architecture

4. End-User Security Awareness

(1) - 4.1 Human Factor in Cyber Security

(2) - 4.2 Phishing and Social Engineering Attacks

(3) - 4.3 Best Practices for User Training

5. Malware Analysis and Defense

(1) - 5.1 Types of Malware and Their Characteristics

(2) - 5.2 Techniques for Malware Analysis

(3) - 5.3 Malware Prevention Strategies

6. Incident Response and Management

(1) - 6.1 Building an Incident Response Plan

(2) - 6.2 Incident Detection and Reporting

(3) - 6.3 Post-Incident Analysis and Recovery

7. Cyber Risk Management

(1) - 7.1 Risk Assessment Processes

(2) - 7.2 Quantitative vs. Qualitative Risk Analysis

(3) - 7.3 Risk Mitigation Strategies

8. Cloud Security Essentials

(1) - 8.1 Understanding Cloud Security Risks

(2) - 8.2 Securing Cloud Applications and Data

(3) - 8.3 Compliance Challenges in the Cloud

9. Cryptography and Data Protection

(1) - 9.1 Fundamentals of Cryptography

(2) - 9.2 Implementing Encryption Techniques

(3) - 9.3 Data Loss Prevention Strategies

10. Securing Internet of Things (IoT)

(1) - 10.1 IoT Security Challenges

(2) - 10.2 Best Practices for IoT Device Security

(3) - 10.3 Case Studies of IoT Attacks

11. Cyber Security Compliance and Regulations

(1) - 11.1 Overview of Key Cyber Security Regulations

(2) - 11.2 The Role of Compliance in Cyber Security

(3) - 11.3 Implementing Compliance Frameworks

12. Advanced Threat Detection Techniques

(1) - 12.1 Anomaly Detection Algorithms

(2) - 12.2 Behavioural Analysis in Cyber Security

(3) - 12.3 Leveraging AI and Machine Learning

13. Security Operations Center (SOC) Functionality

(1) - 13.1 Role of SOC in Cyber Defense

(2) - 13.2 SOC Tools and Technologies

(3) - 13.3 Metrics for SOC Effectiveness

14. Digital Forensics and Investigations

(1) - 14.1 Fundamentals of Digital Forensics

(2) - 14.2 Evidence Collection and Preservation

(3) - 14.3 Conducting Forensic Analyses

15. Future Trends in Cyber Security

(1) - 15.1 Anticipating Cyber Security Challenges

(2) - 15.2 Innovative Technologies in Cyber Defense

(3) - 15.3 Preparing for the Cyber Security Landscape of 2030

1. Introduction to Cyber Security

1.1 The Importance of Cyber Security in 2025

The digital landscape in 2025 is characterized by a range of escalating threats that present significant challenges for both businesses and individual users. Cyberattacks have grown increasingly sophisticated, with hackers utilizing advanced techniques such as artificial intelligence to circumvent traditional security measures. Phishing schemes, ransomware attacks, and data breaches have become more prevalent, causing widespread disruption. These threats not only result in sensitive information loss and financial damage but also undermine an organization's reputation. Individuals are frequently targeted through social engineering tactics that exploit human psychology to extract personal data. As businesses deepen their reliance on digital infrastructures, the stakes of these threats have reached new heights, necessitating robust security measures to mitigate potential risks.

The economic ramifications of cyber incidents are staggering. Organizations experiencing data breaches can incur costs in the millions, covering immediate recovery efforts and long-term remediation. These expenses may include system upgrades, legal fees, and fines for regulatory non-compliance. Additionally, the reputational damage poses a critical concern; customers increasingly prioritize privacy and security, and breaches can lead to a loss of trust that is challenging to restore. Many organizations see their market value significantly affected post-breach, with repercussions lingering long after the incident has been resolved. In an era where online reviews and social media shape public perception, a company's ability to demonstrate strong cyber hygiene can be a deciding factor for consumers when choosing between competing brands. Awareness and proactive measures are essential to mitigate these threats and protect valuable assets.

As cyber threats continue to evolve, it remains crucial for cybersecurity professionals to stay informed about current trends and the strategies employed by attackers. By consistently monitoring and adapting strategies to combat emerging threats, professionals can safeguard their organizations more effectively. Ongoing training, participation in threat intelligence sharing networks, and regular updates to security policies are invaluable practices. Moreover, fostering a culture of security awareness among employees is critical, as human error often represents the weakest link in security measures. Remember, vigilance and preparedness are fundamental defenses in this ever-changing digital landscape.

1.2 Overview of Cyber Threats

Cyber threats come in various forms, with malware, phishing, and ransomware being some of the most prevalent today. Malware, or malicious software, refers to programs designed to harm or exploit any programmable device, service, or network. This category includes viruses, worms, and Trojans that can disrupt operations or steal sensitive data. Phishing, on the other hand, often involves deceptive emails or messages that trick individuals into providing personal information. Attackers craft these communications to appear legitimate, making it easy for unsuspecting users to unwittingly relinquish access to their accounts or even financial information. Ransomware is another significant threat that encrypts a victim's data, demanding payment for its release. Its growing sophistication has made it a favorite tool among cybercriminals, with attacks expanding across various sectors, including healthcare and education.

The motives behind these cyber attacks are diverse and often rooted in both personal and financial gain. Financially motivated attacks are particularly rampant; cybercriminals are continuously seeking ways to pilfer money directly from individuals or organizations. One prevalent form of this is through stealing credit card information or conducting fraudulent transactions. Espionage also drives many cyber attacks, especially in government and corporate sectors where proprietary information can give a competitive advantage. Disruption, on the other hand, targets the operational integrity of systems and networks. Cyber terrorists or hacktivists may aim to cause chaos to send a message or to promote a specific ideology. Understanding these motives is crucial for cyber security professionals, as it allows them to better anticipate the types of threats that may arise and develop effective strategies to combat them.

Staying informed about the latest trends in cyber threats is essential for professionals in this field. Regularly updating protective measures and training staff on recognizing potential phishing attempts or the signs of ransomware can make a significant difference. Sharing intelligence about common tactics used by attackers can also help organizations to fortify their defenses. As threats evolve, so too should the strategies to combat them, creating a proactive rather than reactive approach to cyber security.

1.3 Cyber Security Frameworks and Standards

Widely recognized frameworks such as the NIST Cybersecurity Framework and the ISO/IEC 27001 Standard play a crucial role in the formulation and implementation of effective cybersecurity protocols. These standards provide guidelines that help organizations to safeguard their sensitive information and protect against evolving cyber threats. The NIST framework emphasizes a comprehensive approach, focusing on five core functions: Identify, Protect, Detect, Respond, and Recover. This structure allows organizations to assess their current cybersecurity capabilities and create targeted strategies to address vulnerabilities. On the other hand, the ISO/IEC 27001 Standard lays out the requirements for establishing, implementing, maintaining, and continually improving an information security management system (ISMS). Both frameworks enable organizations to adopt best practices, ensuring that they manage their information security risks in a systematic and efficient way.

These frameworks are vital for risk management and compliance in today's rapidly changing digital landscape. They assist organizations in identifying applicable legal, regulatory, and contractual requirements relating to information security. The integration of such frameworks into corporate governance systems ensures that organizations not only meet the minimum compliance requirements but also enhance their overall security posture. By aligning with these recognized standards, organizations can better anticipate risks and prepare for potential threats—thus minimizing the impact of security incidents. Moreover, the use of standardized frameworks simplifies communication between stakeholders, as it provides a common language and understanding of security practices and expectations. Understanding their relevance in both risk management and compliance helps cybersecurity professionals stay one step ahead of potential threats.

Cybersecurity professionals should consider regularly updating their knowledge of these frameworks, as they evolve to address new threats and technological changes. Keeping abreast of the latest versions of NIST and ISO standards can give professionals a competitive edge in risk assessment and management. Practical application of these standards not only enhances an organization's security landscape but also prepares them for future challenges in compliance and risk governance. Actively engaging with these frameworks empowers professionals to become proactive rather than reactive in preventing cyber incidents.

2. Understanding Threat Landscapes

2.1 Types of Cyber Threats and Vulnerabilities

Cyber threats come in various forms, and understanding them is crucial for anyone in the field of cybersecurity. Common types of cyber threats include malware, phishing, ransomware, and advanced persistent threats (APTs). Malware refers to any software intentionally designed to cause damage to a computer, network, or server. This category encompasses viruses, worms, and spyware, all of which exploit vulnerabilities in systems. Phishing attacks typically involve deceptive emails or messages designed to trick users into providing sensitive information, often leveraging social engineering to increase their effectiveness. Ransomware is a particularly damaging type of malware that encrypts a victim's files and demands payment for their recovery, often exploiting weaknesses in user awareness and system security. APTs represent a more sophisticated threat, typically involving coordinated and prolonged attacks aimed at stealing information or causing disruption to critical systems.

Cybercriminals often exploit specific attack vectors to carry out their malicious activities. Common attack vectors include web applications, email communications, and unsecured networks. Web applications are frequent targets since they are often poorly secured, allowing attackers to exploit coding errors and vulnerabilities to gain unauthorized access. Email remains one of the most effective channels for cybercriminals, as the human element is often the weakest link. They may use social engineering techniques to trick users into clicking on malicious links or downloading infected attachments. Unsecured networks, particularly public Wi-Fi, pose significant risks as attackers can intercept data transmitted over these networks, leading to unauthorized access to sensitive information. Cybersecurity professionals must stay vigilant and regularly update their knowledge on these attack vectors to effectively defend against emerging threats.

Keeping abreast of the current trends in cyber threats and vulnerabilities is essential for maintaining security in any organization. It's important not just to understand the types of threats but also how they evolve. Regularly conducting vulnerability assessments and penetration testing can help identify weaknesses in a network before they can be exploited by attackers. Moreover, ensuring that all software is up-to-date and implementing strong security protocols, such as multi-factor authentication, can significantly reduce the risk of falling victim to these threats. Always remain proactive in your cybersecurity approach; staying informed and prepared is the best defense against the ever-changing landscape of cyber threats.

2.2 Emerging Threat Trends

The landscape of cybersecurity is constantly shifting, with new and evolving threats emerging at an alarming rate. One significant trend is the rise of zero-day exploits, which take advantage of vulnerabilities that are not yet known to the software vendor or the public. These kinds of attacks can be particularly dangerous because there's often no defense or patch available at the time of exploitation. Cybercriminals are becoming increasingly sophisticated, using advanced persistent threats (APTs) to gain prolonged access to a network. APTs often involve a stealthy, multi-phase attack methodology which typically aims to steal data over an extended period instead of making a one-off effort. They are particularly prevalent in sectors such as finance, healthcare, and government, where data is not only valuable but highly sought after.

Emerging technologies are influencing the threat landscape in significant ways, amplifying vulnerabilities while simultaneously providing new tools for defenders. The adoption of cloud computing, for example, introduces novel risks that organizations must understand and mitigate. Misconfigurations in cloud settings can lead to data breaches, as sensitive information may inadvertently become accessible to unauthorized users. Additionally, the proliferation of Internet of Things (IoT) devices expands the attack surface exponentially. Many of these devices are often under-protected, making them appealing targets for attackers looking to infiltrate a network. Artificial intelligence and machine learning are also increasingly being employed both by cybercriminals to automate attacks and by security professionals to enhance their defenses. As more organizations rely on these advanced technologies, understanding the potential downsides becomes essential.

To stay ahead of emerging threats, cybersecurity professionals must continuously educate themselves about the latest trends and techniques used by attackers. Regularly participating in threat intelligence sharing communities can provide valuable insights into new attack vectors. Engaging in red teaming exercises can also help practitioners recognize their organization's vulnerabilities proactively. It's crucial to adopt a mindset of adaptability, as the tactics and tools used in cyberattacks evolve rapidly.

2.3 Real-World Case Studies of Cyber Attacks

High-profile cyber attacks like the 2017 Equifax breach and the 2020 SolarWinds incident have underscored the vulnerabilities that organizations face. The Equifax breach, which exposed personal data of approximately 147 million individuals, resulted from a failure to patch known vulnerabilities. This incident revealed the importance of timely software updates and robust identity protection measures. On the other hand, the SolarWinds attack showcased the dangers of supply chain vulnerabilities, where hackers infiltrated an widely-used software platform which in turn affected numerous organizations, including governmental agencies. These events served as harsh reminders of the intricate nature of cyber threats and the necessity for continuous security assessments. The lessons learned emphasize not only the technical need for better security hygiene but also highlight the importance of a proactive security culture within organizations.

Following such incidents, organizations have had to rethink their incident response strategies. For instance, the immediate response to the Equifax breach involved a call to action to enhance monitoring and implement a comprehensive security framework. Incident response plans have evolved to include threat hunting and incident simulations to better prepare teams for similar events. The SolarWinds compromise prompted many companies to reassess their supply chain security and implement zero-trust models, where every attempt to access resources, whether inside or outside the network, is treated as a potential threat. Effective post-attack strategies are focused on transparency, with impacted organizations often needing to communicate clearly with stakeholders to rebuild trust and outline preventive measures.

The continuous evolution of cyber threats means that security professionals must stay abreast of emerging tactics and techniques used by attackers. Engaging in threat intelligence sharing can offer significant benefits, as organizations learn from others' misfortunes. Investing in advanced detection technologies and employee training ensures that the human element of cybersecurity is not overlooked. Regularly refining incident response plans and conducting tabletop exercises makes organizations more resilient and better prepared to respond effectively when the next cyber attack occurs. Keeping systems updated and investing in advanced monitoring tools are crucial steps that no organization can afford to ignore.

3. Network Security Fundamentals

3.1 Essential Network Security Concepts

Key principles of network security revolve around three critical elements: confidentiality, integrity, and availability, often referred to as the CIA triad. Confidentiality ensures that sensitive information is accessed only by those authorized to see it. This is achieved through various methods, including encryption and access controls. Integrity involves maintaining the accuracy and consistency of data over its lifecycle, preventing unauthorized modifications. Availability ensures that information and resources are accessible to authorized users when needed, requiring robust systems that can withstand attacks and recover from failures. Focusing on these principles lays the groundwork for a secure network, enabling professionals to build defenses against the myriad threats that can compromise these essential elements.

Segmentation and defense in depth are integral strategies that enhance security in complex environments. Network segmentation involves dividing a larger network into smaller, more manageable sections, which limits access and reduces the attack surface. By isolating sensitive data and critical systems, organizations can better control who has access to what information. Defense in depth is the practice of layering multiple security measures throughout the network architecture. Rather than relying on a single mechanism to protect against attacks, this approach uses a combination of firewalls, intrusion detection systems, and other defenses, creating a multi-faceted protective barrier. Together, these concepts enable cybersecurity professionals to not only defend against common threats but also to adapt to the constantly evolving landscape of cyber attacks.

Understanding the principles behind the CIA triad and the strategies of segmentation and defense in depth equips cybersecurity professionals with the necessary tools to mitigate risks and enhance their overall security posture. Keeping abreast of the latest trends, including emerging threats and innovative attack vectors, is crucial. Implementing frequent training and awareness programs can also strengthen team readiness against the ever-changing tactics used by malicious actors.

3.2 Firewalls, IDS/IPS, and Their Roles

Firewalls serve as the first line of defense in network security, acting as a barrier between trusted internal networks and untrusted external networks. Their primary function is to inspect incoming and outgoing traffic and determine whether to allow or block specific traffic based on predefined security rules. This makes them vital in preventing unauthorized access, data breaches, and various cyber threats. Firewalls can be hardware-based, software-based, or a combination of both, allowing organizations to tailor their security measures according to their specific environments and needs. By effectively managing and filtering traffic, firewalls help maintain network integrity and protect sensitive data from external attacks, showcasing their importance in a comprehensive security strategy.

Intrusion Detection Systems (IDS) and Intrusion Prevention Systems (IPS) are crucial components of an organization's defense against cyber threats, but they serve different purposes. An IDS primarily monitors network traffic for suspicious activities and potential security breaches. When an intruder is detected, the IDS generates alerts that inform security personnel of potential threats, allowing for a timely response. On the other hand, an IPS goes a step further by not only detecting threats but also preventing them. It actively analyzes and takes immediate action to block any malicious activity detected within the network. Understanding the distinction between an IDS and an IPS is essential for effective cyber defense. While both systems play critical roles in enhancing security, their differing capabilities and operations mean that skilled professionals must thoughtfully integrate them into their overall security posture to maximize their efficacy.

Staying updated with the latest trends in firewall technologies and IDS/IPS developments is crucial for cybersecurity professionals who aim to counteract evolving threats. Regularly reviewing firewall configurations and IDS/IPS logs ensures that security measures are optimized and threats are quickly neutralized. By fostering a proactive security culture that prioritizes continuous learning and adaptation, organizations can better defend against complex attacks and safeguard their valuable assets.

3.3 Securing Network Architecture

Designing a secure network architecture requires a comprehensive understanding of both hardware and software components that play critical roles in safeguarding the system. Security should be woven into the very fabric of the network and starts from the ground up. Hardware like firewalls, intrusion detection systems, and routers are the frontline defense mechanisms that filter out malicious traffic. Firewalls act as barriers between the trusted internal network and untrusted external networks, blocking unauthorized access while allowing legitimate communication. Meanwhile, intrusion detection systems monitor network traffic for suspicious activity, providing alerts when potential threats are detected. Software security solutions, such as antivirus programs and endpoint protection, are equally vital, as they defend against malware and other cyber threats that could compromise sensitive data. The integration of physical hardware protections with robust software solutions creates a formidable defense, ensuring that vulnerabilities are minimized and breaches are effectively mitigated.

However, building a secure network architecture is not a one-time task; it demands continuous monitoring and proactive adjustments in response to evolving threats. Cybersecurity is a dynamic field where attackers constantly refine their methods, necessitating an agile approach to network security. Regular analyses of network performance and security logs can reveal patterns that indicate potential vulnerabilities or breaches. Adopting a strategy of continuous improvement involves making architectural adjustments based on the intelligence gathered from these assessments. For instance, if a new type of malware or exploit is identified in the wild, tweaking firewall rules or updating intrusion detection systems may be necessary to better protect the network. Staying informed about the latest threats and cyber attack trends empowers cybersecurity professionals to refine their architecture effectively. This vigilance and adaptability ensure that the network remains resilient against emerging threats, safeguarding both the organization and its data.

One practical approach to secure network architecture is the implementation of a layered security model, often referred to as defense in depth. By combining multiple security measures at different levels, the organization can create overlapping layers of protection that enhance overall security. For instance, using strong authentication mechanisms at access points, real-time traffic monitoring, and network segmentation can significantly reduce attack surfaces. Each layer provides an additional barrier to potential intruders and delays their progress, often allowing for early detection and response. Cybersecurity professionals should also consider adopting automated tools for monitoring network performance and security. These tools can help identify anomalies quicker than manual processes, ensuring a rapid response to any changes that might indicate a potential threat. Keeping an agile mindset and embracing innovative solutions are crucial steps in securing network architecture in today's ever-evolving threat landscape.

4. End-User Security Awareness

4.1 Human Factor in Cyber Security

Humans play a pivotal role in cyber security, acting as both potential threats and the first line of defense. Individuals within an organization can inadvertently create vulnerabilities through carelessness, such as clicking on malicious links or using weak passwords. These actions can lead to significant breaches, which expose sensitive data and compromise the overall security posture of the organization. Furthermore, insider threats, whether malicious or accidental, highlight the need for awareness regarding behaviors that may jeopardize security. Employees are often the targets of social engineering attacks, where attackers manipulate them into revealing confidential information. Recognizing that humans are often the weakest link in the cyber security chain underscores the need for continuous education and vigilance in this ever-evolving field.

Building a culture of security awareness within an organization is crucial. This culture starts from the top, where leadership must foster an environment that prioritizes security at every level. Regular training sessions and workshops can engage employees and emphasize the importance of cyber hygiene practices, such as identifying phishing attempts and safeguarding personal data. Encouraging open communication about security concerns empowers staff to report suspicious activities without fear of retribution. Additionally, integrating security awareness into the onboarding process ensures that new hires understand the organization's commitment to security right from the start. When employees feel responsible for cyber security, it transforms them from mere workers into active defenders against potential threats.

Ultimately, developing a proactive approach to cyber security that recognizes the human element is essential. Organizations should implement robust security policies while simultaneously promoting a strong awareness culture. Tools such as simulated phishing attacks can provide real-world experiences, highlighting vulnerabilities in a controlled manner. The goal is not only to protect the organization's assets but also to cultivate informed and alert employees who understand their vital role in safeguarding information. Encouraging a mindset of continuous learning and adaptation in the face of evolving threats positions organizations to better withstand the dynamic landscape of cyber security.

4.2 Phishing and Social Engineering Attacks

Social engineering techniques are at the heart of many cyberattacks, often manifesting as phishing schemes that cleverly exploit human psychology. Attackers employ various tactics, including pretexting, baiting, and impersonation, to manipulate individuals into divulging sensitive information or performing actions beneficial to the attackers. Phishing typically involves emails or messages that appear legitimate, luring users into clicking on malicious links or downloading harmful attachments. These communications often mimic trusted sources, making the deception more convincing. Techniques evolve rapidly, with attackers refining their strategies to create more personalized approaches, such as spear phishing, which targets specific individuals or organizations. This advanced targeting increases the likelihood of success, emphasizing the need for continuous awareness and education among employees regarding these threats.

The psychological tactics employed in these attacks are crucial for understanding their effectiveness. Attackers often exploit emotions such as fear, curiosity, and urgency to compel users to act without thinking. For example, a phishing email may claim that an account has been compromised, creating anxiety that leads the recipient to click on a link without verifying its authenticity. Similarly, messages that induce curiosity, such as unexpected attachments or intriguing subject lines, can catch users off guard. By recognizing these psychological triggers, users can become more vigilant. Awareness of common tactics can make a significant difference. Encouraging a culture of scepticism helps in identifying suspicious communications and motivates individuals to double-check the legitimacy of requests.

To bolster defenses against phishing and social engineering attacks, organizations should prioritize ongoing training and simulated phishing exercises. Regularly educating employees about the latest trends in phishing tactics enhances their ability to identify potential threats. Moreover, incorporating a clear protocol for reporting suspicious emails or messages can create an environment where safety is a shared responsibility. Empowering personnel with knowledge not only protects them individually but also fortifies the organization's overall cyber resilience. Practicing caution and maintaining a sceptical approach towards unsolicited communications can drastically reduce the risk of falling victim to these deceptive strategies.

4.3 Best Practices for User Training

Training users to recognize and respond to cyber threats is a crucial aspect of any cybersecurity strategy. Users are often the first line of defense against attacks, so equipping them with the right knowledge can significantly reduce vulnerabilities. One key strategy is to educate users on the types of threats they might encounter, such as phishing emails, malware, and social engineering tactics. By using real-world examples and case studies, training sessions can become more relatable and impactful. Encouraging an environment where users feel comfortable reporting suspicious activities is also vital. This can prevent potential threats from escalating and reinforce a culture of security within the organization.

Regular updates to training materials are essential because the cyber threat landscape is constantly evolving. As new hacking techniques emerge, training programs need to adapt to include information on the latest threats and prevention measures. Alongside continuous education, implementing simulated phishing tests can provide valuable insights into how users respond to threats. These simulations help reinforce learning by allowing users to experience phishing attempts in a controlled environment, making them more alert and better prepared in real situations. Feedback from these tests can guide further training, addressing gaps in knowledge and awareness.

Lastly, it's beneficial to create a feedback loop where employees can voice their concerns and share experiences related to cybersecurity. This not only reinforces learning but also helps in identifying areas that may require more attention in training. Keeping training engaging and relevant, such as incorporating gamification or competitions, can further enhance user involvement and retention of information. A good practice is to use storytelling in training sessions, making scenarios more personalized and relatable. By taking these steps, organizations can build a resilient workforce that actively contributes to a secure environment.

5. Malware Analysis and Defense

5.1 Types of Malware and Their Characteristics

Malware can be broadly categorized into several types, each with its own unique features and modes of operation. Viruses are one of the most recognized types of malware. They attach themselves to legitimate programs and replicate when the host program is executed. Unlike viruses, worms are standalone malware that can self-replicate and spread independently across networks. Ransomware has gained notoriety for its ability to encrypt a victim's files, demanding payment in exchange for decryption. Trojans disguise themselves as legitimate software, tricking users into executing them without suspicion. Adware and spyware focus on surveillance and ad generation, often compromising user privacy. Understanding the specific characteristics of these types helps cyber professionals develop effective strategies for prevention and response.

The lifecycle of malware typically involves several stages: infiltration, execution, replication, and propagation. During infiltration, the malware gains access to a system, often through deceptive tactics like phishing or exploiting vulnerabilities. Once inside, it executes its malicious code, which can result in data theft, encryption, or corrupting files. Replication occurs as the malware spreads to other systems, whether through email attachments, network shares, or compromised websites. Common propagation methods include social engineering and exploiting security weaknesses in software. By recognizing this lifecycle, cybersecurity professionals can implement more robust defenses and mitigate the impact of potential attacks.

As the landscape of malware continues to evolve, staying informed about the latest trends and attack methods is essential for cybersecurity professionals. New variants are constantly emerging, each designed to outsmart traditional defense mechanisms. For instance, advanced malware can adjust its behaviour based on the environment, making detection challenging. Understanding the characteristics and lifecycle of different types of malware not only aids in effective malware identification but also enhances the ability to respond swiftly to incidents. Regular training and adoption of preventive measures, such as software updates, firewalls, and intrusion detection systems, are crucial in safeguarding against the ever-present threat of malware.

5.2 Techniques for Malware Analysis

Malware analysis is crucial for understanding malicious software behaviour and mitigating the damages it causes. Static analysis refers to the examination of the malware without executing its code. By analyzing the malware's code, file structures, and strings, cybersecurity professionals can gather vital information about its potential capabilities. Static analysis allows analysts to identify indicators of compromise (IOCs), such as IP addresses, domain names, and file hashes, even before the malware is executed. This method can reveal the malware's intended target and its possible functionalities. Although static analysis is powerful, it has limitations; sophisticated malware may obfuscate its code or employ tricks to mislead analysts, which makes further investigation necessary.

Dynamic analysis, on the other hand, involves executing the malware in a controlled environment to observe its behaviour in real-time. This technique can provide insights into how the malware interacts with the operating system and network. During dynamic analysis, analysts can monitor file system changes, registry modifications, and network traffic generated by the malware. It can also help reveal advanced techniques, such as process injection or rootkit capabilities. Combining both static and dynamic analysis offers a more comprehensive view of the malware and enhances the ability to respond to threats effectively.

Sandboxing and reverse engineering are advanced methods that build on these fundamental techniques. Sandboxing involves running the malware in an isolated virtual environment that mimics a real system. This approach allows cybersecurity experts to study the malware without putting actual systems at risk. In a sandbox, the malware can execute freely, enabling analysts to capture its behaviour and actions accurately without interference. This controlled setting is essential for studying more aggressive threats that could lead to broader network compromise if executed on a live system. Reverse engineering, on the other hand, delves deeper into the malware's architecture by disassembling its code. Analysts use decompilers and debuggers to reverse-engineer applications, allowing them to understand the underlying algorithms and potentially identify vulnerabilities that can be exploited to neutralize the malware. Understanding the source and functionality of malware can lead to more effective countermeasures and highlight the need for continuous development of defensive tools.

For effective malware analysis, maintaining an up-to-date forensic toolkit is vital. Incorporate the latest tools and techniques to stay ahead of evolving threats. Exploring new analysis tools will not only enhance your skills but also keep you informed about the latest trends in malware tactics and defenses.

5.3 Malware Prevention Strategies

Proactive measures are essential in safeguarding systems against malware infections. One of the most effective strategies is maintaining regular updates for all software, operating systems, and applications. Updates often include patches that fix vulnerabilities which could otherwise be exploited by malware. Therefore, implementing an automated update system can help ensure that all programs are running the most secure versions available. Additionally, user training plays a critical role in malware prevention. Employees should be educated on the dangers of phishing attacks, suspicious email attachments, and unsafe browsing habits. By fostering a culture of security awareness, organizations can significantly decrease the risk of accidental malware infections originating from user actions.

Endpoint protection solutions are vital for comprehensive malware prevention. These solutions act as the first line of defense against malware and include antivirus programs, anti-malware tools, and endpoint detection and response (EDR) solutions. They continuously monitor devices for malicious activity and can quarantine harmful files before they cause damage. Moreover, network-based prevention techniques complement endpoint solutions by monitoring incoming and outgoing traffic for signs of malware. Firewalls and intrusion prevention systems play a crucial role in these techniques, establishing barriers against potential threats and actively blocking suspicious activity. Implementing a multi-layered security approach that combines endpoint protection with network defenses provides robust coverage against various types of malware.

Incorporating threat intelligence into existing prevention strategies can enhance malware defenses even further. This involves staying informed about the latest malware trends and tactics used by cybercriminals. Sharing information about emerging threats with other organizations can also create a communal defense against potential attacks. Additionally, conducting regular security audits and penetration testing can identify vulnerabilities before they can be exploited. Being proactive and vigilant is key to staying ahead of malware threats, and organizations can also consider employing machine learning algorithms to detect potential threats based on behavioural patterns. This not only reduces response times but also allows for a more dynamic security posture.

6. Incident Response and Management

6.1 Building an Incident Response Plan

An effective incident response plan is essential for organizations facing the evolving landscape of cybersecurity threats. Key components of this plan include clearly defined roles and responsibilities among team members. Each person involved must understand their specific duties during an incident, whether they're in charge of initial detection, communication, analysis, or remediation. Such clarity ensures swift action, minimizing the potential damage from a security breach. Additionally, the involvement of various stakeholders, including IT staff, management, and even legal advisors, can provide a comprehensive approach to incident response. Regular training and simulations can also help reinforce these roles, enabling the team to act confidently and cohesively when real incidents occur.

The importance of regular testing and updating of the incident response strategy cannot be overstated. Cyber threats are constantly evolving, and without continuous assessment, any incident response plan may quickly become outdated. Scheduled drills and tabletop exercises allow the team to practice their responses under controlled conditions, exposing any weaknesses in the plan. Feedback from these sessions should inform updates, ensuring the plan remains relevant. Furthermore, adjusting the strategy based on emerging threats or lessons learned from previous incidents strengthens the organization's ability to respond effectively in the future.

To maintain your organization's readiness, consider establishing a review schedule for your incident response plan. A good practice is to revisit the plan at least once a year or after significant security events. This proactive approach not only helps identify gaps and areas for improvement but also fosters an organizational culture that prioritizes cybersecurity preparedness. Remember, in the world of cybersecurity, being prepared is the best defense against the inevitable incidents that will occur.

6.2 Incident Detection and Reporting

Effective incident detection is the backbone of a strong cybersecurity posture. Among the most essential methods for detecting incidents are log analysis and alerting mechanisms. Logs provide a rich source of information about system activities and user behaviour. Analyzing these logs can reveal patterns and anomalies that indicate potential security breaches. Regularly reviewing logs from firewalls, intrusion detection systems and applications helps identify suspicious activities before they escalate. Implementing automated log analysis tools can enhance this process significantly by identifying unexpected behaviours quickly. Coupled with alerting mechanisms, organizations can receive real-time notifications about potential incidents, enabling them to respond promptly. Properly configured alerts can filter out noise, focusing on significant threats while minimizing false positives, which helps security teams prioritize their responses effectively.

Timely reporting plays a crucial role in incident management. When an incident is detected, its swift reporting is vital for initiating standardized response procedures. Organizations must develop clear protocols for reporting incidents to ensure everyone involved knows their responsibilities. A consistent approach helps streamline the response, facilitating collaboration among various teams, including IT, legal, and public relations. Reporting should include relevant details about the incident, such as the type of attack, the affected systems, and the suspected timeline. Furthermore, a well-defined escalation matrix ensures that critical incidents reach the appropriate leadership quickly, allowing for informed decision-making. This cohesive reporting framework enhances situational awareness and enables organizations to adapt their response strategies based on the severity of the incident.

Following these principles not only strengthens an organization's defenses but also builds resilience against future attacks. As cyber threats evolve, staying up-to-date with detection methods and reporting protocols is essential. Cybersecurity professionals should regularly train their teams on these protocols, conduct mock incident drills, and review past incidents to learn from successes and failures. This continuous improvement approach fosters a proactive security culture, ensuring that the organization is better equipped to handle real-world scenarios with confidence.

6.3 Post-Incident Analysis and Recovery

Conducting a thorough post-incident review is crucial for understanding what went wrong during a cyber event. This process involves gathering everyone who played a role in the incident response, including technical teams, management, and, if necessary, external partners. The goal is to dissect the incident meticulously. Start by documenting the timeline of events, noting every action taken, from the moment the breach was detected to the final steps of mitigation. Consider not just the technological failures that occurred but also human factors. Was there a lack of communication? Were there gaps in knowledge or abilities? Identifying these root causes is key because without understanding the why, organizations risk repeating the same mistakes. Utilize frameworks like the Five Whys or Fishbone Diagram to facilitate deeper analysis, allowing teams to uncover layers of contributing factors. Improving processes and bolstering existing defenses hinges on these learnings, transforming a negative into a positive step forward in cybersecurity maturity.

Recovery from an incident is another vital phase that demands careful attention. The immediate priority is to restore systems to operational status while ensuring data integrity. Begin by executing a rollback to the last known good configuration or restoring from backups, which underscores the importance of robust backup strategies in advance of any attack. As systems come back online, monitoring tools should be employed to verify that no remnants of the threat persist. It's also crucial to communicate with end-users and stakeholders about the steps being taken and to reassure them about the integrity and security of their data. Implementing strategies such as forensic analysis helps in understanding the full impact of the breach, providing valuable insights for both recovery and future prevention. Following restoration, conducting system and network scans will help ensure that no backdoors or additional vulnerabilities remain. This multi-faceted approach not only brings the affected systems back online but also strengthens the overall security posture against future incidents.

In the aftermath of an incident, take the opportunity to refine the incident response plan. Draw on the lessons learned during the post-incident review to update protocols and training materials, ensuring that your team is better equipped to handle similar events in the future. Building a culture that values continuous improvement will further fortify your organization's defenses. Always remember, while threats may evolve, a proactive and informed team, armed with insights from past incidents, stands the best chance of navigating the complex landscape of cyber threats.

7. Cyber Risk Management

7.1 Risk Assessment Processes

Identifying and evaluating cyber risks within organizations requires a structured methodology that aligns with the unique operational landscape of each entity. The first step is to understand the various assets that need protection, including both tangible and intangible resources such as customer data, intellectual property, and critical infrastructure. By employing methods like asset inventory, organizations can prioritize which elements are most crucial to their operations. Once valuable assets are identified, potential threats must be assessed. This involves analyzing various threat vectors, such as phishing attacks or ransomware, that could exploit vulnerabilities in the system. A critical component of this evaluation process is the likelihood of each threat occurring and the potential impact it may have on the organization. This comprehensive risk evaluation enables organizations to develop a profile of their risk exposure, which is essential for prioritizing remediation efforts.

To effectively perform risk assessments, there are several tools and techniques available that help streamline the evaluation process. One popular option is quantitative risk analysis, which calculates risk using numeric values that quantify the impact and likelihood of threats. This method is particularly useful for organizations looking to derive concrete data to justify security investments. Alternatively, qualitative methods can offer valuable insights when numeric data is scarce. Tools such as the Common Vulnerability Scoring System (CVSS) can be instrumental in benchmarking vulnerabilities within systems and applications. Furthermore, taking advantage of automated tools allows organizations to continuously monitor their environments and generate reports that highlight areas of concern. This proactive approach helps in identifying new vulnerabilities emerging from software updates or changes in the network. It is vital for cybersecurity professionals to stay informed about emerging tools and advancements that can enhance the effectiveness of their risk assessment processes.

Regular and comprehensive risk assessments not only bolster an organization's security posture but also contribute to a culture of awareness regarding cybersecurity threats. Incorporating risk assessments into the overall cybersecurity strategy ensures that organizations are not only prepared to respond to existing threats, but also resilient against future ones. A useful practice is to schedule assessments on a regular basis and after significant changes to the IT environment, such as new technology implementation or personnel shifts. Cybersecurity professionals should always be on the lookout for the latest threats and ensure that their risk assessments are relevant to the current threat landscape.

7.2 Quantitative vs. Qualitative Risk Analysis

The differences between quantitative and qualitative approaches to risk analysis play a crucial role in how cyber security professionals assess potential threats to their organization. Quantitative risk analysis involves numerical assessments, where risks are calculated in monetary terms or probabilities. This approach provides a concrete measurement of risk levels, enabling professionals to prioritize risks based on their potential financial impact. For instance, if a specific vulnerability in a system could potentially lead to a loss of $100,000, a quantitative analysis would give clear guidance on which vulnerabilities require immediate attention based on potential cost. In contrast, qualitative risk analysis focuses more on the subjective assessment of risks, relying on expert judgment and experience rather than hard numbers. It categorizes risks as high, medium, or low based on their nature and perceived impact. This qualitative approach is beneficial in scenarios where data is scarce, allowing professionals to make informed decisions based on qualitative criteria like reputation damage or customer trust, which are less easily quantified.

The choice between quantitative and qualitative risk analysis often hinges on the specific goals of the organization and the resources available. When a security team has access to a wealth of data, such as historical loss figures or detailed incident reports, quantitative analysis can provide a precise understanding of risks, making it especially suitable for organizations with significant budgets allocated to risk management. However, in environments where data is limited or the costs of detailed analysis outweigh the benefits, qualitative analysis can be more effective. It allows for a quicker and more flexible approach, enabling teams to adapt to rapidly evolving threats, which is particularly important in the dynamic field of cyber security. Additionally, organizations with limited risk management resources may find qualitative assessments easier to implement, as they do not require extensive data collection or complex mathematical models.

Understanding the nuances of these methods is essential for cyber security professionals aiming to stay ahead of current trends in risk management. Applying both approaches in a complementary manner can provide a more holistic view of risk. For example, using qualitative analysis initially to identify potential risks can then inform a more focused quantitative assessment of the highest-priority areas. This blended strategy allows professionals to leverage the strengths of both methods, ensuring that resources are used efficiently while maintaining a robust defense against cyber threats. Additionally, staying informed about emerging trends and real-world threats can enhance risk analysis efforts, helping professionals make better predictions about potential vulnerabilities and their impacts.

7.3 Risk Mitigation Strategies

Effective risk mitigation strategies are essential for managing the landscape of cybersecurity threats. Organizations employ a combination of technical and administrative controls to mitigate risks they have identified. Technical controls refer to the use of technology and software to secure networks, systems, and data. This includes firewalls, intrusion detection systems, and encryption. These tools act as barriers against potential attacks, safeguarding sensitive information from unauthorized access. Meanwhile, administrative controls involve policies and procedures that govern how an organization operates. This encompasses employee training, incident response plans, and access control measures to ensure that personnel are educated about potential risks and know how to respond in a security incident. A comprehensive approach combines these strategies to create multiple layers of protection that enhance overall security posture.

Continuous monitoring plays a pivotal role in the risk management process. As cyber threats evolve, the environment surrounding an organization changes rapidly, necessitating an adaptive risk management approach. Continuous monitoring involves the ongoing assessment of the security posture, which allows organizations to detect anomalies and vulnerabilities in real-time. By implementing tools that provide alerts on suspicious activities and automated responses to potential breaches, organizations can respond swiftly to mitigate damages. This dynamic process enables cybersecurity professionals to remain proactive rather than reactive, allowing for the identification of trends that could signify emerging threats. The adoption of continuous monitoring not only strengthens defense mechanisms but also fosters a culture of vigilance and preparedness.

The importance of integrating these risk mitigation strategies cannot be overstated. Staying informed on the latest cybersecurity trends and threats is crucial for cybersecurity professionals. Engaging with threat intelligence platforms, subscribing to relevant security briefs, and participating in industry conferences are practical ways to keep knowledge fresh. Additionally, fostering a culture of collaboration within organizations can enhance the effectiveness of risk mitigation efforts. Sharing insights and experiences across teams can help identify potential weaknesses and develop more robust strategies. By remaining vigilant and adaptive, cybersecurity professionals can significantly lower the probability and impact of cyber threats, ensuring that their organizations are better protected.

8. Cloud Security Essentials

8.1 Understanding Cloud Security Risks

Cloud computing brings numerous advantages, including flexibility and scalability, but it also introduces specific security risks that need careful consideration. One of the most significant risks is data breaches, where sensitive information can be accessed by unauthorized individuals. These breaches can occur due to vulnerabilities within the cloud provider's infrastructure or through improper configurations by users. Additionally, compliance issues arise as organizations must navigate a complex landscape of regulations, such as GDPR and HIPAA, which mandate strict controls over data handling and protection. Failure to comply not only exposes organizations to potential fines but can also damage their reputation and lead to a loss of customer trust.

The shared responsibility model is fundamental to understanding cloud security. This framework clarifies the roles and responsibilities between cloud service providers and customers. While providers ensure the security of the cloud infrastructure, customers must manage the security of the applications and data they place within that cloud. This means that even in a secure cloud environment, customers are not absolved from their responsibility to implement proper security measures like encryption and access controls. Misunderstandings about this model can lead to gaps in security, with customers believing that the provider is wholly responsible for securing their data, which is far from the truth. Awareness of this shared responsibility is crucial for enhancing security posture in cloud deployments.

Understanding these risks and responsibilities is essential for cybersecurity professionals. They need to stay informed about the evolving threat landscape in the cloud environment. Regularly assessing the security protocols in place, conducting penetration testing, and utilizing advanced encryption can significantly reduce the likelihood of data breaches. Cybersecurity experts must also remain vigilant about compliance requirements and ensure their organizations' practices align with legal mandates. Taking a proactive stance and continuously updating the security strategy will help navigate the complexities associated with cloud security risks.

8.2 Securing Cloud Applications and Data

Securing applications hosted in the cloud requires a comprehensive understanding of the unique challenges posed by this environment. Best practices begin by implementing robust identity and access management solutions. This entails not only ensuring that only authorized users have access but also regularly reviewing permissions to prevent any unnecessary exposure. Multi-factor authentication (MFA) is crucial, as it adds an extra layer of security beyond just passwords. Utilizing security groups and roles can further streamline access control and minimize the chances of unauthorized access. It is essential to keep software up to date, as vulnerabilities are often targeted once discovered. Implementing a rigorous patch management policy ensures that all applications and services are fortified against known threats. Additionally, monitoring for unusual activity in real-time can give security teams vital insights that help them respond to potential attacks swiftly.

Data encryption plays a critical role in protecting sensitive information in cloud applications. Encrypting data both at rest and in transit is necessary to guard against interception or unauthorized access. Encryption keys must be managed carefully, ideally using a dedicated key management system that adheres to best practices, including regular rotation and secure storage. Alongside encryption, precise access controls are fundamental to safeguarding sensitive data. Role-based access control (RBAC) ensures that users can only access the data necessary for their tasks. This limits exposure in the event of a breach, as any accessed data will likely be less sensitive than it could be if broader access was allowed. Audit trails should be maintained to keep track of who accessed what information and when, providing accountability and aiding in compliance efforts.

Staying ahead of emerging threats in the cloud requires continuous education and adaptation. Cybersecurity professionals should regularly engage in training sessions and stay updated on the latest trends, tools, and techniques used by malicious actors. Participating in forums, attending conferences, and subscribing to cybersecurity publications can provide insights into real-world attack scenarios and new mitigative technologies. Engaging in penetration testing can also uncover vulnerabilities before they are exploited, ensuring that defenses are as strong as possible. A proactive approach to security will not only help protect cloud applications and data but also foster a culture of vigilance that is vital in today's dynamic threat landscape.

8.3 Compliance Challenges in the Cloud

The regulatory landscape impacting cloud security and data privacy is continually evolving, presenting significant challenges for organizations operating in this space. Various regulations such as GDPR, HIPAA, and CCPA impose strict requirements for data handling, and non-compliance can lead to hefty fines and reputational damage. These regulations mandate not only how data is stored but also how it is accessed and shared across different jurisdictions. As organizations turn to cloud solutions, the responsibility of ensuring compliance shifts, often leading to confusion over who holds accountability between the cloud service provider and the organization itself. Understanding the regulatory requirements specific to the organization's industry and geographical location is crucial. Many regulations also require rigorous data encryption, regular audits, and comprehensive breach notification procedures, which can complicate operations and increase overhead costs.

To navigate these compliance challenges, organizations should adopt a proactive approach. Implementing clear policies for data management is essential, along with regular training for employees on compliance obligations and best practices. Employing the principle of least privilege can help limit access to sensitive data, thus minimizing risk. Regular audits and assessments of cloud configurations ensure that compliance measures are being adhered to in real-time. Additionally, utilizing third-party compliance tools can provide organizations with visibility into their cloud environments, allowing them to quickly identify and rectify potential compliance gaps. Organizations should also ensure that third-party vendors are compliant with the same regulations, as they can significantly impact your own compliance status. Building strong communication channels between compliance teams and IT departments can further facilitate a culture of compliance across the organization.

The complexity of compliance in the cloud can be overwhelming, but staying informed about regulatory changes and technological advancements can give organizations a competitive edge. Investing in ongoing education for cybersecurity professionals who manage cloud environments is vital, as this fosters a deeper understanding of compliance intricacies. It can be beneficial to create a centralized compliance dashboard, allowing for real-time monitoring and rapid response to compliance risks. Always ensure that your cloud service provider is transparent about their compliance measures and can provide detailed documentation regarding their practices. A well-prepared organization is not only better equipped to navigate the regulatory landscape but also builds a reputation of reliability and trust with its clients.

9. Cryptography and Data Protection

9.1 Fundamentals of Cryptography

Cryptography is an essential element in the realm of cybersecurity. It revolves around several key concepts, including keys, algorithms, and different types of encryption. At its core, cryptography involves transforming information so that only authorized individuals can understand it. Keys are essentially strings of bits that determine the output of a cryptographic algorithm, which can be likened to a lock and key mechanism. The algorithms dictate how data is converted from plaintext, which is readable, into ciphertext, which is scrambled and unreadable. This transformation can occur through various encryption types, such as symmetric encryption, where the same key is used for both encryption and decryption, and asymmetric encryption, which employs a pair of keys—one public and one private. The choice of algorithm and key length influences the complexity and security of the encryption, making it crucial for cybersecurity professionals to stay educated on current methodologies and best practices.

The role of cryptography extends far beyond mere data privacy; it also secures communications between individuals and systems. It underpins essential technologies such as secure web browsing, email encryption, and virtual private networks (VPNs). By ensuring that data remains confidential and unaltered during transmission, cryptography builds trust in online transactions and communication channels. As cyber threats continue to evolve, understanding how to effectively employ cryptographic techniques becomes increasingly important. For example, as we see surges in man-in-the-middle attacks and phishing schemes, robust encryption serves as a proactive defense against the interception and compromise of sensitive information.

Staying ahead of potential vulnerabilities requires not only knowledge of the fundamentals but also awareness of emerging trends in cryptography and cybersecurity. This includes being familiar with the implications of quantum computing on traditional encryption methods, as well as advancements in post-quantum cryptographic algorithms designed to withstand such threats. Cybersecurity professionals should regularly engage with ongoing research and developments in the field, enabling them to effectively combat new hacking techniques while maintaining data integrity and confidentiality. A practical tip for professionals is to implement multi-layered security measures that combine strong cryptographic practices with other security protocols, ensuring a fortified defense against diverse cyber threats.

9.2 Implementing Encryption Techniques

Encryption is crucial in protecting sensitive data, and several methods exist to achieve this. Symmetric encryption, where the same key is used for both encoding and decoding data, is popular for its speed and efficiency in scenarios like database encryption. AES (Advanced Encryption Standard) is a widely used symmetric algorithm due to its robust security features and fast processing times. In contrast, asymmetric encryption employs a pair of keys – one public and one private. This method is beneficial for secure communications over untrusted networks, as it allows secure key exchange without the need for the sharing of secret keys. RSA and ECC (Elliptic Curve Cryptography) are well-known asymmetric algorithms widely used for securing email communications and digital signatures. Additionally, hashing techniques like SHA-256 ensure data integrity by producing a fixed-size hash value unique to the given data, making it ideal for verifying the authenticity of files and passwords.

However, implementing encryption effectively comes with its challenges. One significant hurdle is key management. Without proper key management practices, the very encryption intended to protect data can turn into a vulnerability. Best practices include using hardware security modules (HSMs) for key storage, implementing strong access controls, and regularly rotating keys to minimize risks. Moreover, organizations must balance convenience and security when deploying encryption, as overly complex systems can lead to user errors. Awareness about potential limitations, such as the performance impact of encryption on system resources, is essential; understanding the proper trade-offs will enable security professionals to deploy encryption without sacrificing efficiency. Regular training for employees about encrypted data handling and security policies also enhances overall security posture.

It's important to stay updated with the latest encryption trends and vulnerabilities as cyber threats evolve continuously. Keeping abreast of new algorithms and patches for existing encryption technologies can prevent security breaches caused by outdated practices. Participate in forums and subscribe to security newsletters to remain informed. Remember that while encryption is a powerful tool, it should be part of a layered security strategy, including firewalls, intrusion detection systems, and user education, to create a comprehensive defense against current and emerging cybersecurity threats.

9.3 Data Loss Prevention Strategies

Data breaches and unauthorized access have become increasingly prevalent in today's digital landscape. Organizations are now focusing on leveraging a combination of technologies and practices to safeguard sensitive information effectively. Data Loss Prevention (DLP) tools play an essential role in this effort. These tools utilize various techniques such as content discovery, monitoring, and data classification to detect and prevent potential leaks of sensitive data, whether through email, web applications, or physical devices. Machine learning algorithms are often integrated to enhance the accuracy and efficiency of these systems, enabling them to identify anomalies that may indicate a breach attempt. Overall, implementing an effective DLP strategy ensures that organizations can mitigate risks associated with data loss and reinforce their security posture against evolving cyber threats.

While technologies are vital, policy development is equally crucial in establishing a comprehensive data loss prevention strategy. Policies serve as the foundation upon which organizations build their security practices. A well-defined data governance policy outlines roles and responsibilities, access controls, and acceptable use guidelines, setting clear expectations for employees and stakeholders. Additionally, regular training and awareness programs are essential for educating staff about potential threats and the importance of data security. Engaging employees not only fosters a culture of security but also helps to identify vulnerabilities that may not be apparent to IT professionals alone. By prioritizing policy development, organizations can create a robust DLP framework that not only protects data but also empowers employees to be proactive in defending against data loss.

Continuous assessment and adaptation of both technologies and policies are necessary to keep pace with emerging threats. Regular audits and penetration testing can help organizations identify weaknesses in their security frameworks, allowing for timely updates and improvements. Furthermore, staying informed about the latest attack vectors and tactics employed by cybercriminals is essential for maintaining an effective DLP strategy. Cybersecurity professionals should participate in relevant training, forums, and information-sharing platforms to stay ahead of the curve. Incorporating a proactive approach to data loss prevention not only secures data but also enhances overall trust in the organization's ability to protect sensitive information.

10. Securing Internet of Things (IoT)

10.1 IoT Security Challenges

Securing IoT devices and networks presents unique challenges that differ significantly from traditional IT security. One of the primary difficulties is the sheer number of connected devices. Each IoT device serves as a potential entry point for attacks, creating a vast attack surface that is hard to monitor and defend. Many IoT devices are designed with minimal computing power and memory, which limits their ability to run sophisticated security software. Consequently, manufacturers often prioritize functionality and cost-efficiency over security, leading to vulnerabilities that can be easily exploited. Furthermore, the lack of standardization across the IoT landscape compounds these issues. Different devices may have varying security protocols, making it difficult to implement a cohesive security strategy. This fragmentation can create loopholes that cybercriminals exploit, often taking advantage of outdated software and firmware that many devices do not regularly receive updates for. The proliferation of devices also complicates identity and access management, as traditional methods of user authentication may not be suitable for the unique nature of IoT devices.

The implications of poor IoT security extend far beyond the immediate theft of personal data or unauthorized access to devices. These vulnerabilities can have cascading effects on broader network security. An insecure IoT device can serve as a foothold for attackers, allowing them to infiltrate larger networks and systems, often facilitating attacks on critical infrastructure. For example, a compromised smart thermostat could potentially allow hackers to gain access to a building's internal network. Once inside, they could launch more sophisticated attacks, including data breaches or ransomware incidents. Additionally, the interconnected nature of IoT devices means that one weak link can compromise an entire network, leading to widespread disruptions. Such breaches not only threaten data integrity but can also damage an organization's reputation and trustworthiness, incurring significant financial losses. As organizations increasingly rely on IoT systems for operational efficiency, recognizing and mitigating the risks associated with these devices becomes crucial. Cybersecurity professionals must therefore adopt a proactive approach to monitor vulnerabilities, ensuring that all IoT devices are secured and that systems are revised in light of emerging threats.

A practical tip for cybersecurity professionals dealing with IoT security challenges is to implement regular security assessments of all connected devices. This includes evaluating their firmware for updates, ensuring strong password policies are enforced, and isolating IoT devices on separate networks whenever possible. By doing so, even if one device is compromised, the potential damage to critical systems can be minimized. Establishing a comprehensive IoT security strategy that includes not just detection and reaction protocols but also proactive measures is essential for maintaining robust network security in an increasingly interconnected world.

10.2 Best Practices for IoT Device Security

Securing IoT devices throughout their lifecycle is essential to protect sensitive data and maintain the integrity of networks. The security process starts from the moment a device is conceived, continuing through its deployment, use, and eventually decommissioning. During the design phase, it is crucial to incorporate security by default. This means applying strong encryption techniques, utilizing secure boot mechanisms, and ensuring that devices have a unique identity. Manufacturers must prioritize these features to prevent vulnerabilities from the outset. As devices are deployed, establishing a secure configuration is also vital. Implementing best practices such as changing default passwords, disabling unnecessary features, and ensuring secure communication protocols play a significant role in hardening devices against attacks.

The lifecycle management of IoT devices doesn't end with configuration. Regular updates and monitoring are paramount in maintaining security. Software updates should be streamlined to ensure devices frequently receive the latest security patches and upgrades to guard against newly discovered vulnerabilities. This includes both firmware and application-level updates. Devices that do not receive timely updates can quickly become targets for attackers. Continuous monitoring of IoT devices is equally important. Employing automated tools to track device behaviour can help identify unusual patterns that may indicate a security breach. Regular assessments and audits should also happen to ensure devices remain compliant with security policies, thereby reducing risks.

Building a comprehensive approach to IoT security requires collaboration between manufacturers, service providers, and end-users. Educational programs aimed at users should emphasize the significance of IoT security practices, including how to maintain secure environments. End-users must understand the responsibility they have for keeping device software updated and monitoring their network for potential threats. A final practical tip is to establish a detailed incident response plan covering IoT devices. This plan should address preventive measures, detection methods, and response strategies to ensure swift action can be taken if a security incident occurs. Such proactive measures can lead to a more resilient IoT ecosystem.

10.3 Case Studies of IoT Attacks

High-profile IoT attacks have highlighted various vulnerabilities that cyber criminals exploit to breach systems. One notable incident was the Mirai botnet attack in 2016, which turned unsecured IoT devices, like cameras and printers, into a massive network of bots used to launch powerful Distributed Denial of Service (DDoS) attacks. This event not only disrupted many services but also laid bare the weak security protocols in IoT devices, such as default passwords and lack of firmware updates. Another prominent attack is the 2019 Ring camera hack, where attackers gained access to users' live feeds, exposing security inadequacies in device configurations and the significance of data protection. These incidents serve as a chilling reflection of how unprotected devices can be leveraged to compromise user privacy and safety, showcasing a lack of robust authentication measures and the consequences of overlooking security during the device design phase.

The lessons derived from these incidents are crucial for shaping future IoT security strategies. First and foremost, it's vital to prioritize strong, unique passwords for every device, steering clear of default settings that make an easy target for attackers. Additionally, regular firmware updates are essential to patch any known vulnerabilities and ensure that devices are secured against evolving threats. Awareness and education play a pivotal role in preventing such breaches; users must understand the importance of securing their networks and devices. Furthermore, manufacturers should aim for transparency regarding their security practices, providing users with updates and guidance on best practices for device management. By integrating security from the device's inception and fostering a community of informed users, the IoT landscape can shift toward a more secure future, mitigating risks while enabling innovation.

For cybersecurity professionals, staying vigilant about emerging threats and adopting a proactive approach in their security frameworks is essential. Engaging in continuous education and awareness around current vulnerabilities will empower network operators to better defend against potential attacks. Engaging with industry updates and exploiting online resources to keep abreast of the latest hacking tactics can mitigate risks associated with IoT devices. Collaborative efforts between manufacturers and security experts to enhance IoT security standards will also play a critical role in establishing a safer ecosystem. By sharing insights and experiences from incidents, we can create robust defenses against the persistent challenge of securing IoT devices.

11. Cyber Security Compliance and Regulations

11.1 Overview of Key Cyber Security Regulations

Cybersecurity regulations play a crucial role in protecting sensitive data and maintaining trust in digital systems. Major regulations like the General Data Protection Regulation (GDPR) and the Health Insurance Portability and Accountability Act (HIPAA) set high standards for data privacy and security. GDPR, which came into effect in 2018, imposes strict guidelines on data handling across the European Union, mandating that organizations obtain explicit consent before collecting personal data and offering individuals rights over their information, including the right to be forgotten. Non-compliance can lead to severe penalties, highlighting the importance of organizations prioritizing data protection. Similarly, HIPAA governs the handling of medical information in the United States, mandating that healthcare providers and organizations implement safeguards to ensure the confidentiality and integrity of health data. Together, these regulations demonstrate a shift towards greater accountability in data management, emphasizing that compliance is not merely a legal obligation but also a vital component of risk management.

The variability in regulatory compliance across different regions creates both challenges and opportunities for organizations operating globally. While regulations such as GDPR set a robust standard, other regions may lack similar frameworks, leading to discrepancies in data protection practices. This inconsistency can pose risks for multinational corporations that must navigate a complex landscape of laws and regulations while ensuring that they meet local compliance requirements. For example, Japan has its own data protection law, which is less stringent than GDPR but still requires businesses to take measures to safeguard personal information. Failure to adequately address these global differences can result in significant legal and financial repercussions, not to mention reputational damage. As cyber threats evolve rapidly, understanding the regulatory environment and its implications is paramount for cybersecurity professionals. Staying informed about these regulations enables organizations to implement effective security measures that not only comply with the law but also enhance their overall security posture.

Being aware of key cybersecurity regulations and the variations across different jurisdictions can help professionals tailor their approaches to data security. Regular training sessions on compliance and security best practices can foster a culture of awareness and vigilance within an organization. Engaging with legal experts who specialize in data protection law may also provide valuable insights that can help organizations navigate the complexities of compliance. Recognizing that cybersecurity is a dynamic field with constantly evolving regulations encourages organizations to build robust strategies that can adapt to changes in the legal landscape, ultimately supporting their mission to safeguard sensitive data.

11.2 The Role of Compliance in Cyber Security

Compliance serves as a cornerstone in establishing a solid security posture. In today's digital landscape, the threats we face are ever-evolving, and organizations are frequently challenged to keep pace with these changes. Compliance standards establish a framework for organizations to follow, which helps to mitigate risks and strengthen defenses against cyber threats. When companies adhere to these standards, they not only protect sensitive data but also enhance their reputation in the marketplace. Clients and partners often look for businesses that have a strong compliance record as a sign of reliability and trustworthiness. This relationship between compliance and security is evident; effective compliance fosters a culture of security awareness and proactive measures, making it harder for cybercriminals to exploit vulnerabilities.

Compliance frameworks serve as invaluable guides in cyber security efforts. By providing methodologies and best practices, these frameworks help organizations understand the specific steps they need to take to protect their data and systems. Frameworks such as ISO 27001, NIST Cybersecurity Framework, and GDPR not only outline essential security controls but also offer clear processes for assessing risks and implementing necessary safeguards. Cybersecurity professionals who are familiar with these frameworks can leverage them to align their security strategies with industry standards, creating transparency and accountability. Moreover, these compliance models are adaptable and can be tailored to fit the unique circumstances of an organization, which allows for a more comprehensive approach to security.

Staying compliant and informed about the latest regulations and frameworks will significantly enhance any cybersecurity strategy. Professionals should engage in regular training and assessments to ensure their organization meets compliance requirements while remaining agile in the face of new threats. Having a centralized compliance management system can provide insights into areas of vulnerability that need immediate attention. By integrating compliance into your cybersecurity framework, you not only fortify your defenses but also create a resilient organizational culture that embraces security as a continuous priority.

11.3 Implementing Compliance Frameworks

Implementing compliance frameworks requires a well-structured approach. Organizations can start by understanding the specific regulations or standards that apply to their industry. This might involve researching frameworks such as NIST, ISO 27001, or GDPR, depending on the business sector. The next step involves conducting a thorough gap analysis to identify current compliance levels and areas needing improvement. Collaboration among departments is crucial; IT, legal, and management must work together to create a comprehensive compliance strategy. Training staff on compliance requirements also plays an essential role, as human error often leads to breaches. Regular communication about compliance policies helps create a culture of responsibility within the organization, ensuring that everyone understands their role in maintaining compliance. Establishing clear documentation processes aids in tracking compliance efforts and provides a reference during audits.

Ongoing assessment is vital for maintaining compliance as regulations change and new risks emerge. Organizations should implement a regular review schedule to evaluate their compliance status. This can be achieved through internal audits or assessments by third-party specialists to gain an unbiased perspective. Real-time monitoring tools can also help organizations detect compliance deviations immediately, allowing for swift corrective actions. Additionally, updating compliance frameworks to reflect changes in regulations or business processes is necessary. This includes revising documentation and re-training employees as needed. Staying ahead in compliance involves being proactive rather than reactive. By fostering a continuous improvement mindset, organizations can adapt to the dynamic landscape of cybersecurity threats and compliance requirements.

For practical implementation, consider integrating compliance checks into daily operations. This means creating automated workflows for compliance tasks that minimize manual intervention and errors. Automation not only enhances efficiency but also provides a consistent application of compliance measures across the organization. Regular feedback from staff on the effectiveness of compliance procedures can lead to valuable insights for improvements. Furthermore, utilizing emerging technologies such as artificial intelligence and machine learning can bolster compliance efforts by predicting potential compliance risks and providing recommendations for proactive measures. By embedding compliance into the organizational culture, companies position themselves not only to meet legal requirements but also to build the trust of clients and stakeholders.

12. Advanced Threat Detection Techniques

12.1 Anomaly Detection Algorithms

Anomaly detection is a vital concept in the field of cybersecurity, serving as a frontline defense mechanism against various cyber threats. It revolves around the ability to identify deviations from the norm within a data set. Anomalies can indicate a range of issues, from system malfunctions to external attacks from cyber adversaries. With the rise of sophisticated tactics that cybercriminals employ, understanding these deviations is crucial for cybersecurity professionals. Timely detection of these irregularities can prevent data breaches, minimize losses, and bolster the overall security architecture of an organization. As such, anomaly detection is not just a theoretical tool; it is an essential practice aimed at safeguarding digital infrastructure in our increasingly interconnected world.

Various algorithms have been developed to facilitate effective anomaly detection, each tailored for specific scenarios in threat detection. For instance, statistical methods like Z-score, which quantify how far a data point deviates from the mean, are useful for identifying intrusions in network traffic. Machine learning techniques, such as clustering algorithms like k-means or hierarchical clustering, can group similar data points together and effectively highlight outliers that may represent a threat. More advanced methods, such as Isolation Forest and One-Class SVM, learn patterns from a data set, allowing them to pinpoint anomalies that might otherwise go unnoticed. Each algorithm has its strengths and weaknesses, and choosing the right one often depends on the specific characteristics of the data and the context in which it is being applied.

Staying up-to-date with these algorithms and their applications is crucial for cybersecurity professionals seeking to defend against the evolving landscape of cyber threats. For effective anomaly detection, it is important to continually train models with fresh data to adapt to changing attack patterns and improve accuracy. Regularly reviewing and adjusting detection criteria in light of new intelligence and emerging threats can make a significant difference in an organization's security posture. Incorporating these methodologies with continuous monitoring can provide a robust defense mechanism that not only reacts to threats but also anticipates them.

12.2 Behavioural Analysis in Cyber Security

Behavioural analysis is a powerful tool in the realm of cyber security, particularly when it comes to identifying abnormalities in user behaviour that may indicate potential security breaches. By establishing a baseline of normal activities for users within an organization, security teams can leverage data analytics to monitor real-time behaviour. For instance, if an employee typically accesses files only during business hours, any file access in the middle of the night could raise a red flag. Such deviations might suggest that an account has been compromised or that malicious activity is taking place. Behavioural analysis serves as a proactive measure, allowing organizations to detect anomalies early and respond swiftly to avoid significant damage to sensitive information.

The integration of machine learning into behavioural analysis significantly enhances its accuracy and effectiveness. Machine learning algorithms can process vast amounts of data to identify patterns and correlations that might not be immediately apparent to human analysts. These algorithms continuously learn from ongoing activities, allowing them to refine their understanding of normal behaviour over time. As the system learns, it becomes better equipped to distinguish between benign deviations—like a user working late for a special project—and signs of security threats. This capability not only streamlines incident response but also reduces the number of false positives, enabling security teams to focus their resources on legitimate threats that require immediate attention.

Incorporating behavioural analysis into your cyber security strategy means consistently updating and calibrating your algorithms to match the changing landscape of user behaviour and threat tactics. To optimize your behavioural analysis systems, consider scheduling regular reviews of the baseline activities and engaging in cross-departmental collaboration to encompass a wider range of user activities. This practice will keep your defenses robust and your analysis relevant. Additionally, staying updated on the latest developments in machine learning will empower you to enhance your organization's capability to detect and respond to new types of cyber threats swiftly and effectively.

12.3 Leveraging AI and Machine Learning

Integrating artificial intelligence (AI) and machine learning (ML) into threat detection systems has become a transformative approach in cybersecurity. These technologies enable security systems to analyze vast amounts of data at speeds and volumes that human analysts simply cannot match. By employing algorithms that learn from historical data, systems can identify patterns and anomalies that may indicate a threat. For instance, machine learning models can be trained on known threat behaviours, allowing these systems to evolve and adapt as new threats emerge. This ongoing learning capability is particularly valuable in the rapidly changing landscape of cyber threats, where attackers are constantly developing new methods to bypass defenses. Furthermore, AI can automate repetitive tasks, allowing cybersecurity professionals to focus on more strategic concerns.

However, the use of AI and ML in cybersecurity is not without its challenges and ethical dilemmas. One major concern is the potential for bias in training data, which can lead to false positives or negatives. If the algorithms learn from skewed or incomplete data, they may misinterpret benign activities as malicious, resulting in unnecessary alerts and wasted resources. Moreover, the lack of transparency in how these models operate raises ethical questions regarding accountability when a system fails. If an AI system makes a poor judgment call, determining liability can be complex, especially when relying on black-box algorithms that offer little insight into their decision-making processes. It is crucial for cybersecurity professionals to remain aware of these ethical considerations as they implement AI technologies. Regular audits and the development of guidelines about the ethical use of AI in cybersecurity can help navigate the murky waters of responsibility and ethics in this field.

As cybersecurity professionals adopt these advanced technologies, one practical tip is to ensure they maintain a balanced approach by combining human intuition with machine intelligence. While AI and ML provide powerful tools for threat detection and response, human oversight is essential for validating findings and making nuanced decisions. Training teams to understand the capabilities and limitations of AI systems can enhance the effectiveness of these solutions. Regularly updating training data and refining algorithms will also be vital to counteract any emerging biases and to keep defenses sharp against evolving threats.

13. Security Operations Center (SOC) Functionality

13.1 Role of SOC in Cyber Defense

The primary functions and responsibilities of a Security Operations Center, or SOC, revolve around monitoring, detecting, and responding to cybersecurity incidents. A

SOC serves as the nerve center for an organization's cybersecurity efforts, providing a systematic approach to manage and mitigate risk. Analysts within the SOC work tirelessly to monitor security alerts from various tools and technologies, including firewalls, intrusion detection systems, and endpoint protection solutions. They analyze incoming data, prioritize incidents based on severity, and determine the best course of action. This real-time monitoring is crucial; it allows organizations to catch threats before they escalate into significant breaches that could compromise sensitive data or disrupt business operations.

Beyond just monitoring, SOCs are essential for proactive incident response. When a potential threat is detected, SOC analysts initiate predefined protocols that may involve isolating affected systems, gathering evidence, and mitigating risks. This proactive response minimizes damage and reduces recovery time. By conducting regular threat hunting exercises, SOCs can also develop a deeper understanding of the tactics and techniques employed by cybercriminals. These insights empower organizations to strengthen their defenses and implement strategic improvements to their security posture. Moreover, effective collaboration with other departments, like IT and compliance, ensures that security considerations become an integral part of the overall organizational strategy, enhancing resilience against future attacks.

Engaging in threat intelligence gathering and sharing is another critical aspect of a SOC's role. By staying ahead of emerging threats and understanding the latest vulnerabilities, SOC teams can adjust their strategies accordingly. This ongoing education and adaptation foster a proactive security culture within the organization. Cybersecurity professionals working within a SOC should continuously hone their skills and adapt to the rapidly changing cyber landscape. A practical tip for SOC teams is to leverage automated tools where possible to relieve some of the workload, allowing analysts to focus on more complex tasks and strategic planning, ultimately enhancing the overall efficiency and effectiveness of the cybersecurity efforts.

13.2 SOC Tools and Technologies

Security Operations Centers (SOCs) leverage an array of essential tools for monitoring, detection, and response to cyber threats. These tools are designed to integrate seamlessly, offering SOC analysts a comprehensive view of an organization's security posture. For monitoring, Security Information and Event Management (SIEM) systems play a pivotal role. They collect and aggregate log data from various sources, providing real-time analysis that enables quick detection of suspicious activities. Additionally, Intrusion Detection Systems (IDS) and Intrusion Prevention Systems (IPS) act as critical layers of security, identifying potential threats and automatically responding to incidents. Endpoint Detection and Response (EDR) tools focus on devices, offering advanced threat detection capabilities by analyzing endpoint activity and responding to incidents swiftly. Moreover, threat intelligence platforms provide SOC teams with actionable insights to stay ahead of adversaries by analyzing potential threats and vulnerabilities. Together, these tools create a robust framework for proactive security measures that help organizations defend against evolving cyber threats.

The landscape of SOC technology is continuously evolving, shaped by rapid advancements that enhance their capabilities. Machine learning and artificial intelligence are at the forefront of this transformation, allowing SOCs to automate threat detection and response processes. By employing algorithms that learn from historical data, these technologies can identify anomalies and pinpoint potential threats much faster than traditional methods. Cloud-based security solutions are also emerging, enabling SOCs to scale their operations efficiently and respond to incidents in real-time, regardless of location. The integration of automation into regular SOC operations can streamline workflows, reduce human error, and enable analysts to focus on more complex tasks that require human judgment. Furthermore, the rise of Security Orchestration, Automation and Response (SOAR) platforms helps bridge various security tools, allowing them to communicate and respond cohesively during incidents. As organizations embrace these technological advancements, SOCs will become even more agile and capable of addressing sophisticated threats in an interconnected digital landscape.

Keeping abreast of the latest trends in SOC tools and technologies is crucial for cybersecurity professionals. Regularly engaging with industry publications, attending webinars, and participating in training sessions on newly developed solutions can enhance knowledge and preparedness. It is important to test and evaluate new tools within your specific environment, ensuring they align well with existing security protocols and meet organizational needs. One practical tip is to fostering collaboration among security teams and departments, as sharing insights and experiences can uncover better ways to utilize available technologies, ultimately strengthening the overall security framework.

13.3 Metrics for SOC Effectiveness

Key performance indicators, or KPIs, are essential for measuring the performance and effectiveness of a Security Operations Center (SOC). They provide quantifiable metrics that can guide teams to make informed decisions. Some critical KPIs for a SOC include incident response time, the number of incidents detected and resolved, the mean time to detect (MTTD), and the mean time to respond (MTTR). Monitoring these metrics helps in understanding how quickly a SOC can react to threats and whether it is improving over time. Additionally, metrics like false positive rates and the percentage of successfully mitigated threats provide context on the quality of the SOC's operations. By correlating these KPIs with historical performance data, a SOC can establish baselines that facilitate goal setting and performance reviews, allowing teams to see the impact of their strategies and configurations on overall security posture.

Continuous improvement is crucial in the ever-evolving landscape of cybersecurity threats. To leverage SOC metrics for improvement, organizations can implement a continuous feedback loop. This involves regularly analyzing KPIs to identify trends and patterns that highlight areas requiring enhancement. Adopting frameworks such as the Deming Cycle (Plan-Do-Check-Act) can systematically guide these efforts. For example, if data reveals a high rate of false positives, the SOC can reassess its detection rules and methodologies. Furthermore, regular training and simulations ensure that SOC analysts are well-prepared and equipped to handle new types of threats. An effective strategy also includes utilizing threat intelligence to better inform SOC processes, ensuring that metrics not only reflect past performance but also proactively guide future strategies. Implementing a culture of continuous improvement means that teams are not just reactive but become increasingly proactive against emerging cyber threats. Remember, the key to an effective SOC is not just measuring performance, but actively using these measurements to drive strategic enhancements.

14. Digital Forensics and Investigations

14.1 Fundamentals of Digital Forensics

Digital forensics is a vital discipline that involves the recovery and investigation of material found in digital devices, which is essential in today's technology-driven landscape. At its core, digital forensics is built upon several key principles that guide professionals in their efforts to uncover and analyze evidence. One of the most fundamental concepts is the chain of custody, which refers to the process of maintaining and documenting the handling of evidence from the moment it's collected until it is presented in court. This meticulous documentation ensures that the evidence remains untarnished and can be verified as authentic, making it crucial for legal proceedings and for maintaining the integrity of investigations. Following strict protocols not only enhances the credibility of the findings but also safeguards against challenges that may arise during litigation.

The role of digital forensics in investigating cyber incidents cannot be overstated. In an era where cyber threats are rampant, understanding how to effectively analyze digital evidence is key to identifying and mitigating attacks. Forensics provides the methodologies needed to exonerate the innocent, hold the guilty accountable, and restore systems after breaches occur. Through diligent analysis of digital footprints, passwords, logs, and other data, forensic professionals can reconstruct events leading up to an incident, revealing intentions and methods used by attackers. This meticulous work aids organizations in enhancing their security measures and response strategies, leading to a stronger defense against future threats.

Additionally, as cyber threats evolve, digital forensics must adapt to new technologies and techniques employed by malicious actors. For cyber security professionals, staying updated on the latest forensic tools and methodologies is imperative. By leveraging advanced forensic tools, one can efficiently sift through vast amounts of data and uncover critical evidence previously hidden. Regular training on new digital forensics techniques not only prepares professionals for real-world investigations but also creates a culture of proactive security awareness within organizations. Ensuring that forensic practices are ingrained in the security strategy can significantly improve defense against cyber incidents.

14.2 Evidence Collection and Preservation

Proper protocols for collecting and preserving digital evidence are essential in forensic investigations. When approaching a scene of a digital crime, investigators should follow established guidelines to ensure the evidence's integrity and validity. This involves first assessing the environment where the evidence resides. Investigators must secure the scene to prevent any unauthorized access or alterations. The use of write blockers is crucial when handling storage devices, as these tools enable access to data without changing it. It is also important to document everything meticulously, including the steps taken, the tools used, and the condition of the evidence when it was collected. Maintaining a clear chain of custody from the moment the evidence is obtained until it is submitted in court protects against any claims of tampering or mishandling.

Challenges faced in ensuring evidence integrity during investigations can be numerous and complex. One significant issue involves the rapid evolution of technology, which can lead to variances in data formats and storage methods. Cybercriminals often deploy strategies that actively delete or encrypt evidence upon detection, making it critical for investigators to act swiftly and decisively. Furthermore, human error presents another challenge. Even experienced professionals can inadvertently alter data during collection. Environmental factors such as power failures or interruptions can also impact the evidence if not anticipated. Developing a thorough understanding of the digital landscape is crucial for cybersecurity professionals. Implementing robust training and utilizing specialized forensic software can help mitigate these risks. Staying updated on the latest trends in hacking techniques is equally important, as it empowers professionals to anticipate potential threats to evidence integrity.

For effective evidence collection and preservation, professionals should prioritize continuous education and practice simulacra of evidence collection scenarios. Regular drills ensure that all team members are familiar with protocols and can function effectively under pressure. Always remember that thorough documentation and a proactive approach towards understanding current digital landscapes are your best tools in preserving evidence integrity.

14.3 Conducting Forensic Analyses

Analyzing digital evidence in the context of forensic investigations involves a systematic approach to uncovering relevant data that supports the case at hand. This process typically begins with the identification of potential sources of evidence, such as computers, mobile devices, servers, and cloud storage. Once these sources are identified, forensic professionals use methods like imaging and duplication to create exact copies of the data without altering the original files. These copies enable detailed analysis while preserving the integrity of the evidence. Common analysis techniques include keyword searches, data carving, and timeline analysis, which help to reconstruct events leading up to security incidents. The ability to examine file metadata and system logs also plays a pivotal role in establishing timelines and identifying anomalies that could indicate malicious activity or unauthorized access.

There is a variety of tools available for conducting forensic analysis, each designed to assist analysts in different aspects of the investigation process. Popular forensic toolkits include EnCase, FTK, and X1 Social Discovery, which facilitate in-depth examination of data and provide user-friendly interfaces for navigating complex datasets. These tools are essential for tasks such as recovering deleted files, analyzing network traffic, and capturing volatile data from live systems. The role of these tools extends beyond just data recovery; they also help in documenting findings and generating reports that can be used in legal proceedings. Additionally, open-source solutions, like Autopsy and The Sleuth Kit, have gained traction among forensic experts due to their cost-effectiveness and flexibility, allowing analysts to customize their workflows based on specific case requirements.

Staying informed about the latest technological advancements and emerging threats is crucial for professionals in the field of cybersecurity and digital forensics. As new vulnerabilities arise and cybercriminals evolve their tactics, it's important that forensic analysts continuously update their skill sets and toolsets. Engaging in professional networks, attending conferences, and enrolling in specialized training courses can provide insights into current trends and best practices. One practical tip is to regularly participate in case studies and simulations that replicate real-world hacking scenarios. This hands-on experience not only sharpens investigative skills but also enhances the ability to respond effectively to live incidents.

15. Future Trends in Cyber Security

15.1 Anticipating Cyber Security Challenges

As we delve deeper into the cyber landscape, the potential threats and vulnerabilities that lurk within are becoming increasingly sophisticated. Cybercriminals are continuously refining their techniques, leveraging advanced technologies like artificial intelligence and machine learning to exploit weaknesses in digital infrastructures. The rise of the Internet of Things (IoT) adds another layer of complexity, as each connected device can serve as an entry point for attackers. Vulnerabilities in software, including zero-day exploits, threaten organizations that might not be prepared for rapid response and recovery. Moreover, the shift towards remote work models has expanded the attack surface, exposing firms to new risks associated with unsecured home networks and personal devices. Keeping vigilant against these evolving threats requires a proactive and adaptive mindset, recognizing that yesterday's solutions may not be adequate for tomorrow's challenges.

To effectively safeguard against these imminent challenges, organizations need to adopt comprehensive and proactive measures. Implementing a robust risk assessment framework is crucial, allowing entities to identify their unique vulnerabilities and understand their threat landscape better. Regular training and awareness programs for employees are vital, as human error remains one of the primary causes of security breaches. Additionally, organizations should invest in next-generation firewalls, intrusion detection systems, and advanced endpoint protection to enhance their cyber defense posture. Collaborating with cybersecurity experts and sharing threat intelligence across sectors can also help in staying ahead of emerging threats. Embracing a culture of continuous improvement and readiness will empower organizations to adapt to changing cyber terrains.

Staying informed is not just beneficial; it is essential. Cybersecurity professionals can benefit greatly from subscribing to relevant industry updates, attending cybersecurity conferences, and participating in forums where the latest trends, tools, and techniques are shared. Establishing a routine of reviewing and updating security protocols and ensuring compliance with international standards keeps the organization prepared and resilient against future attacks. Focus on building a response plan that prioritizes quick recovery, as this not only minimizes damage but also reinforces trust among clients and stakeholders. Remember, in the evolving world of cyber threats, the best offense is often a good defense grounded in preparedness and adaptability.

15.2 Innovative Technologies in Cyber Defense

Emerging technologies such as blockchain and artificial intelligence (AI) are reshaping the landscape of cybersecurity. Blockchain offers a decentralized and immutable way to record transactions, making it particularly valuable for securing sensitive data and authenticating identity. Its inherent design helps to mitigate risks like unauthorized access and data tampering. For instance, organizations are exploring the use of smart contracts on blockchain systems to automate processes securely, ensuring that transactions only occur when certain criteria are met. This technology can enhance transparency and trust among parties, which is crucial in sectors like finance and healthcare, where data integrity is paramount. On the other hand, AI systems play a transformative role in threat detection and response. By leveraging machine learning algorithms, these systems can analyze vast amounts of data to identify anomalies that could signify a cyberattack. AI can learn from previous incidents, thereby improving its ability to adapt and respond to new threats in real time. For example, threat intelligence platforms utilizing AI can continuously monitor network activities, flagging unusual behaviours that require immediate attention, thus reducing the time to detect and respond to potential breaches.

The integration of these innovative technologies is having profound impacts on traditional cyber defense mechanisms. Traditional approaches often involve static defenses such as firewalls and signature-based detection systems that can quickly become outdated against sophisticated attacks. With the introduction of AI, organizations can adopt a more proactive defense posture. AI's predictive capabilities allow security teams to anticipate attacks before they occur, shifting the focus from reactive measures to preventive strategies. Similarly, blockchain's decentralized nature reduces the single points of failure that are inherent in conventional systems, making it harder for attackers to achieve their objectives. However, while these technologies provide advanced security features, they also pose new challenges. For example, the complexity of integrating AI into existing systems can lead to vulnerabilities if not implemented properly. Furthermore, as blockchain and AI evolve, the threat landscape adapts as well, with attackers finding new methodologies to exploit these technologies. Hence, cybersecurity professionals must remain vigilant, continuously updating their knowledge and strategies to mitigate the risks associated with these advancements.

To effectively leverage these innovative technologies in cyber defense, it is essential for security professionals to stay informed about the latest developments and real-world applications. Engaging with industry forums, attending relevant workshops, and collaborating with tech innovators can provide deeper insights into best practices and emerging trends. Applying a mixed approach that combines traditional methods with new technologies could enhance overall security posture and resilience against cyber threats. This synergy not only bolsters defenses but also encourages a culture of continuous learning and adaptation within security teams.

15.3 Preparing for the Cyber Security Landscape of 2030

The cybersecurity field is on the brink of significant transformations projected for 2030, driven by advancements in technology and the evolving tactics of cybercriminals. As we look ahead, we can expect the rapid adoption of artificial intelligence and machine learning to streamline threat detection and response.

These technologies will empower professionals to analyze vast amounts of data quickly, identifying patterns and anomalies that could indicate security breaches. However, the flip side is that cybercriminals will also leverage these tools to execute more sophisticated attacks. The implications are clear: cybersecurity professionals must anticipate a future where they are not only defenders of systems but also strategic thinkers able to outsmart increasingly adept adversaries.

Continuous learning is no longer optional; it's a necessity in a landscape that changes at breakneck speed. Cybersecurity professionals need to adopt a mindset of lifelong education, ensuring they stay abreast of the latest trends, threats, and technologies. This involves not just formal education through certifications and training but also engaging with the cybersecurity community through forums, webinars, and conferences. Being proactive in understanding emerging tools and tactics, such as zero trust architectures and next-generation firewalls, will equip professionals with the knowledge needed to counter new threats effectively. By embracing adaptability and resilience as core attributes, cybersecurity experts can thrive in this dynamic environment.

One practical way to maintain relevance in the ever-evolving cybersecurity landscape is to establish a routine of personal development that incorporates both technical skills and soft skills. Practicing coding, systems analysis, or penetration testing alongside enhancing communication and teamwork abilities will create a well-rounded cybersecurity professional. Being knowledgeable in technical areas is essential, but the ability to convey complex information understandably and collaborate can often make the difference in effectively mitigating potential risks. Engaging in local cybersecurity groups or online platforms can foster connections that lead to shared insights, guiding professionals through the complexities of anticipated changes in their field.

www.ingramcontent.com/pod-product-compliance
Lightning Source LLC
LaVergne TN
LVHW081807050326
832903LV00027B/2136